Classical Guitar

Introductory Repertoire and Exercises

by Paulo Oliveira

© 2021 by FretZone Music Publishing

Nashville, TN

ISBN: 978-1-7374515-0-1

Table of Contents

Table of Contents, cont'd

Introduction

Welcome! My intent with this book is to present material targeted toward guitar students in the early stage of their musical journey. In this book, students will encounter an exciting repertoire, coupled with exercises that serve to develop technique and improve fretboard knowledge.

This is not a method book; rather, it is a compilation of pieces and exercises that address a variety of technical and musical issues crucial to the development of every guitarist. The needs of each student should be considered when studying specific repertoire and exercises within this book. As such, the guidance of a teacher is highly recommended through this process.

When selecting repertoire for this book, I sought to find a balance between the inclusion of different periods and styles in the history of the guitar, as well as include some of my favorite contemporary pedagogical works. I am confident that these new pieces and studies will be a unique addition to the student's repertoire. While there are limitations when it comes to the scope of this selection, it is my hope to provide the student with some degree of awareness regarding the major stylistic traits throughout the history of the instrument.

I am honored to include selected studies written by Paulo Porto Alegre, which are not only fine compositions, but also effective pedagogical tools for the development of the aspiring guitarist. The addition of pieces by Celso Delneri and José Ricardo are cause for enthusiasm, as they have a well-measured blend of simplicity and charm. I am also excited to be sharing my "Five Rock Impressions," which are short compositions written for pedagogical purposes; each of them targets a specific technical element, which is briefly described under the title. As a bonus, I included a section at the end of the book with chord voicings and rhythmic patterns for those interested in basic accompaniment techniques for jazz and bossa nova.

Acknowledgments

I would like to give a special thanks to Paulo Porto Alegre, Celso Delneri, and José Ricardo for allowing me to include their wonderful compositions in this publication. To Amorim Lopes, for his beautiful artwork on the cover. To Dan Landes, Robbie Chan, Nick Huff, Francis Perry, Robert Thompson and Jennifer Graybill for their precious help and support throughout this process. I also owe a debt of gratitude to my students and colleagues at Belmont University for inspiring me to make this book a reality.

Part I: 12 Elementary Studies by Paulo Oliveira

"If you are not willing to learn, no one can help you.
If you are determined to learn no one can stop you."

Zig Ziglar

12 Elementary Studies

Paulo Oliveira

Block Chords
Walking Bass
(always)

Melody and Bass

Slurs

Part II: 25 Selected Studies by Paulo Porto Alegre

"We are what we repeatedly do."

Aristotle

25 Selected Studies

Paulo Porto Alegre

(b. 1953)

III
Moderato
p i a p i m p m
1
2
To
p i a p i m p a
m i m i p m p m
D.C. al ⊕ with repetition
Movido
IV
p p p i m a
simile...
Fine
D.C. al Fine with repetition
Thumb
V
m
i
p p
p
a
i
i
m m m m i
i
p
i i a
m
0
p

VI

Block Chords

VIII

Chords
Contraction of 4th finger
i m a i m a
Moderato
m
i
p p p p p p p p simile...

IX

X

XI

Moderato

m i m p i m i m p i p
simile...
simile...
a m i a m p i m a m p i p
XII
Movido
a m i a m i simile...
p p
Fine
D.C. al Fine with repetition

XIII

Moderato

XIV

**Melody on the Bass
and Rolled Chords**

XV

XVI

XVII

Ascending Slurs

XVIII

Descending Slurs

XIX

Ostinato

XX

Prelude with Arpeggios and Slurs

XXI

Ascending Slurs

XXII

Descending Slurs

XXIII

XXIV

XXV

Part III: 5 Rock Impressions by Paulo Oliveira

"Success isn't owned, it's leased.

And rent is due every single day."

J. J. Watt

Pulse

Chord Study

Paulo Oliveira

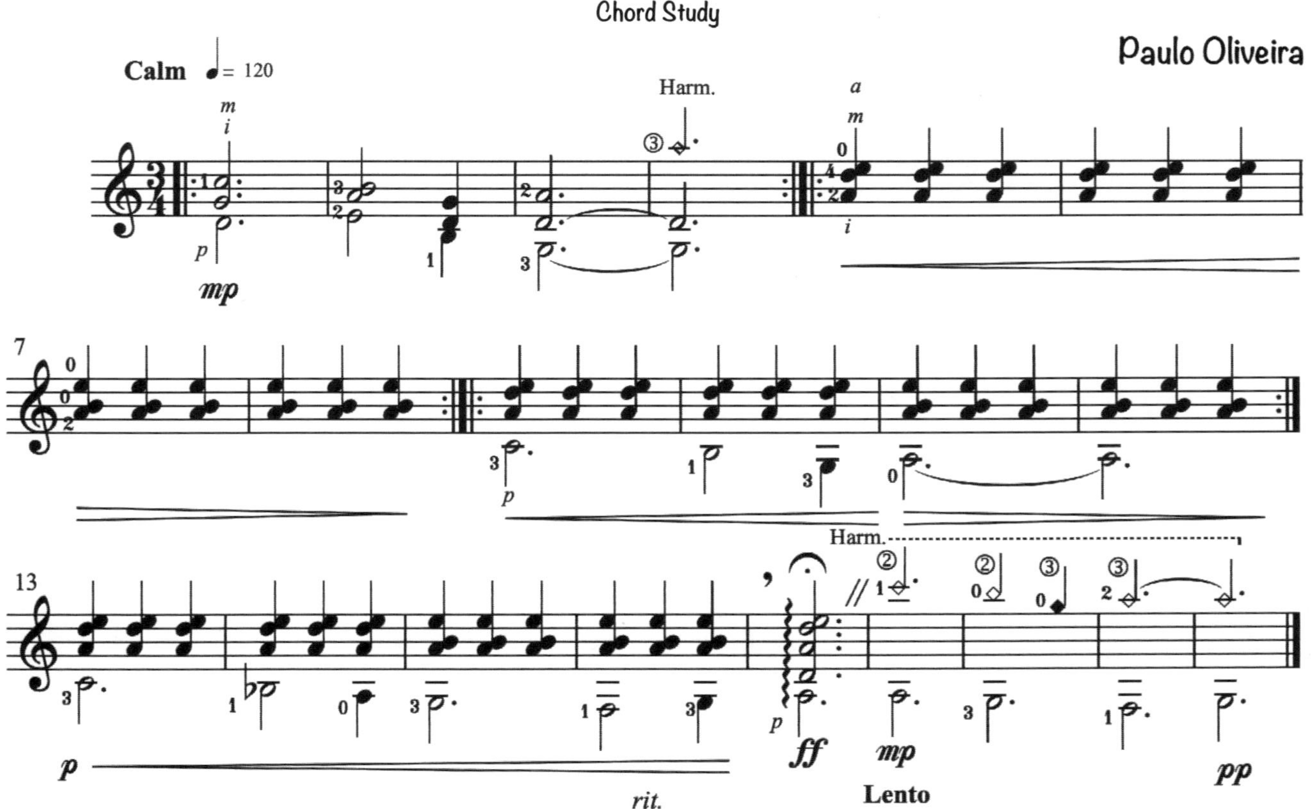

Smokey Canon

Polyphonic Study

Paulo Oliveira

* Denotes the entrance of a new voice

Son of Life

Arpeggios and odd meter

Paulo Oliveira

Power-Chord Study

Chords and Slurs

Paulo Oliveira

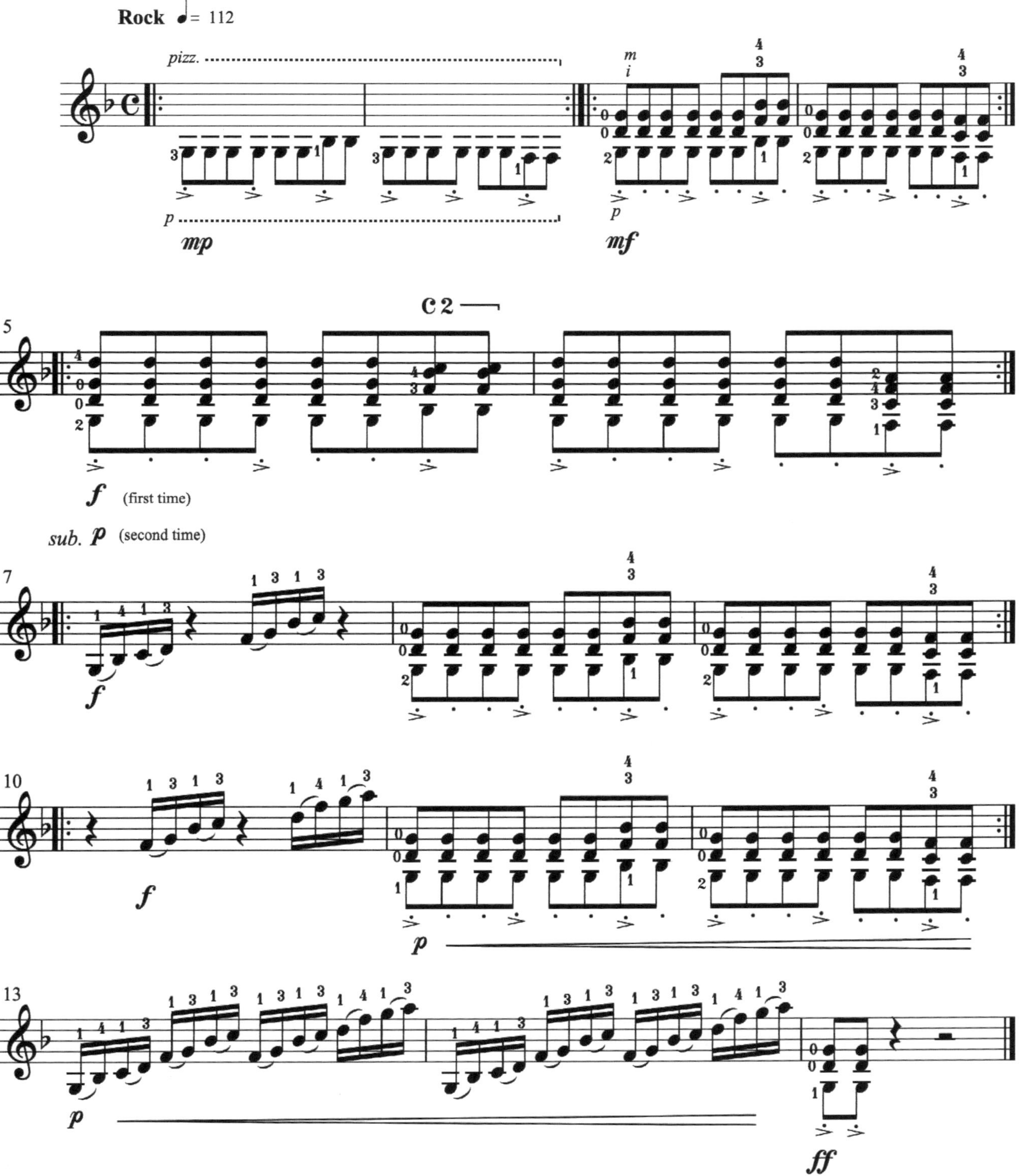

Skinner

Slur Study

Paulo Oliveira

Part IV: Selected Repertoire Pieces and Studies

> "There are no shortcuts to anyplace worth going."
>
> John Maxwell

Green-Sleeves

Anonymous
Renaissance

©2021 FretZone Music Publishing

The Parlement

From the Dowland Manuscript

Anonymous
Renaissance

Pavana I

From El Maestro (1536)

Luis Milan

(1500-1561)

13
15
18
f
m i m i m i
4 1
p
20
23
25
mf
27
poco rit.

Pavana III

From El Maestro (1536)

Luis Milan
(1500-1561)

41
49
55
61
68
74
80

Mrs. Winter's Jump

John Dowland
(1562-1626)

La Dessine

Santiago de Murcia
(1673-1739)

Entrée

From Partita

G. A. Brescianello
(1690-1758)

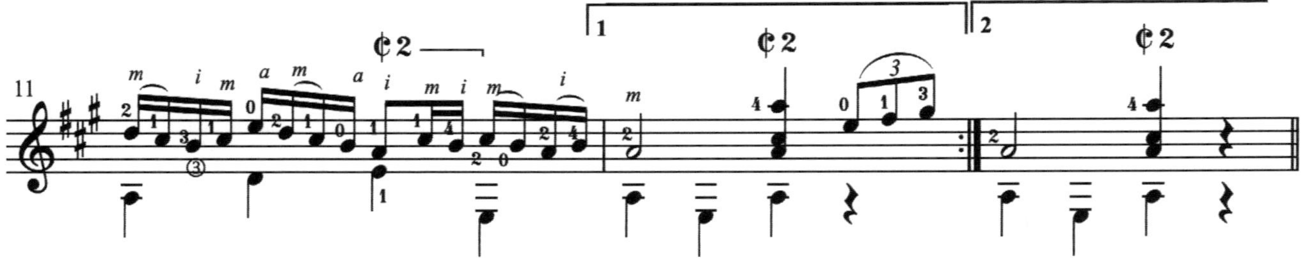

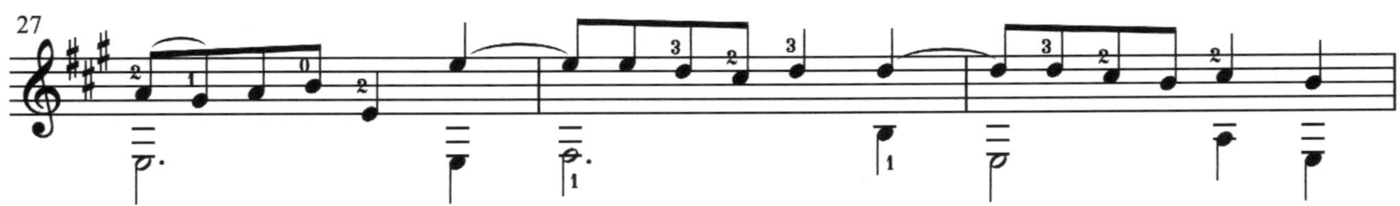

Minuet

From the Notebook for Ana Magdalena Bach

J. S. Bach
(1685-1750)

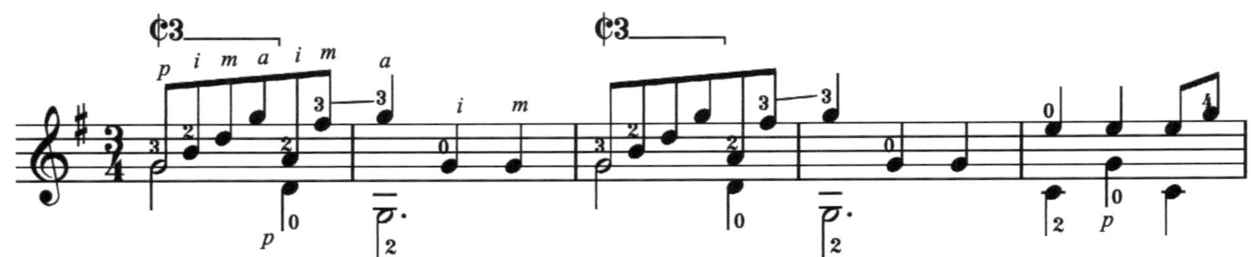

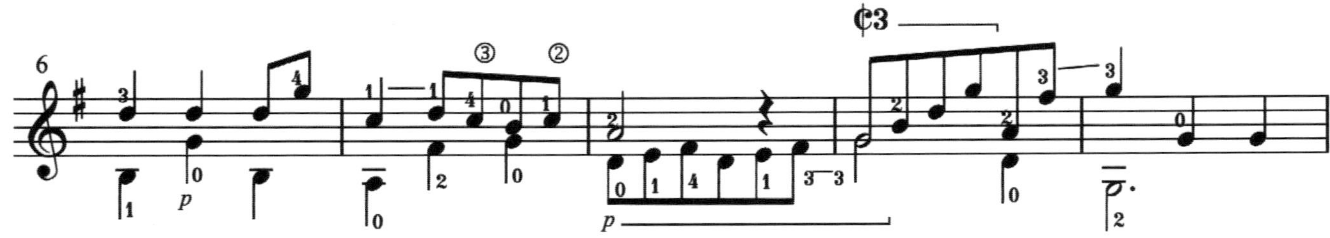

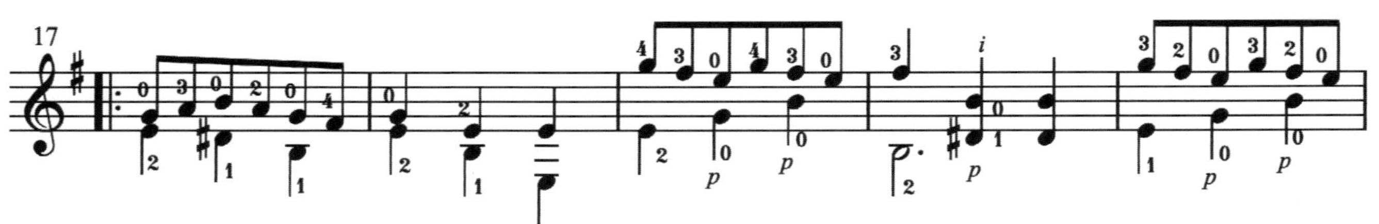

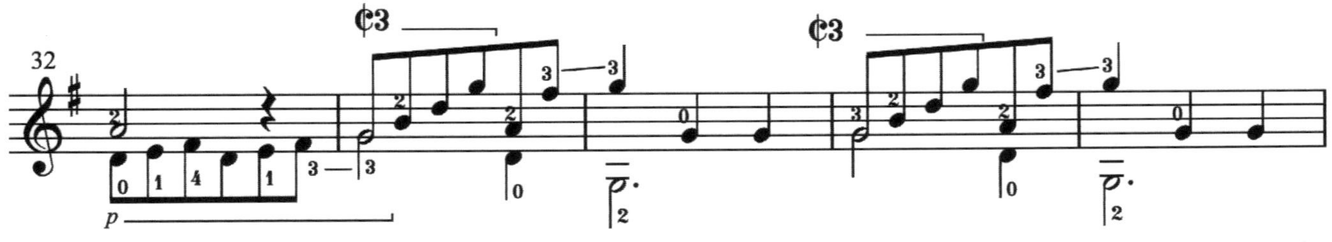

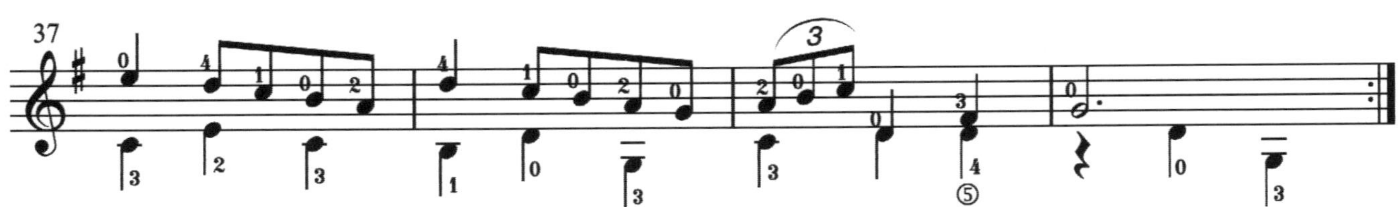

Minuet

From Partita

G. A. Brescianello
(1690-1758)

Andantino
Op.59

Matteo Carcassi
(1792-1853)

Moderato
Op. 39, n.15

Anton Diabelli
(1781-1858)

Andantino

Mauro Giuliani
(1781-1829)

Study in A Minor

Napoleon Coste
(1805-1883)

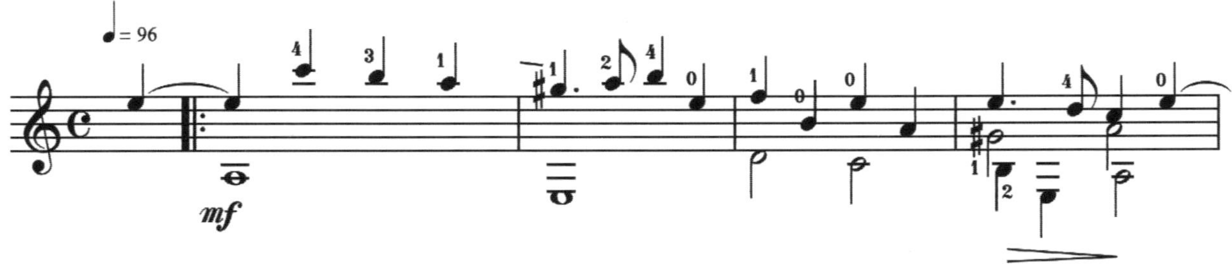

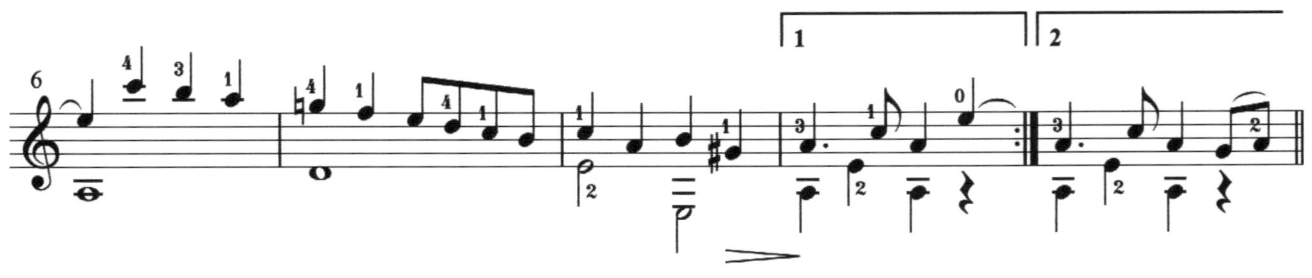

Study no. 3
Op. 60

Matteo Carcassi
(1792-1853)

Study no. 7

Op. 60

Matteo Carcassi

(1792-1853)

Ländler

Op. 9, no. 4

Johann Kaspar Mertz
(1806-1856)

21
sfz
f
rit.
25
p
i a i p i
p
29
i m a
f
i m a
i m a m
a m i
m
rit.
33
p a tempo
37
i m a
¢7
f
p

Galop

Op. 39, no. 8

Matteo Carcassi

(1792-1853)

Study

Op. 31, no. 2

Fernando Sor

(1778-1839)

Lágrima

Francisco Tárrega
(1852-1909)

Study in C Major

Francisco Tárrega
(1852-1909)

Romance de Amor

Study in E Minor

Anonymous

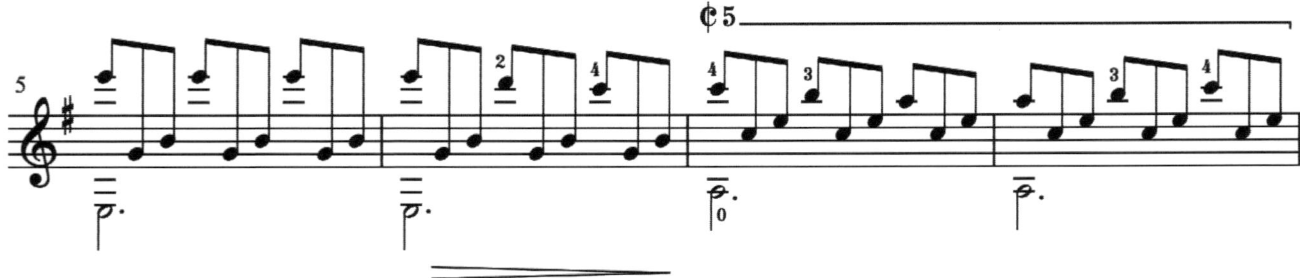

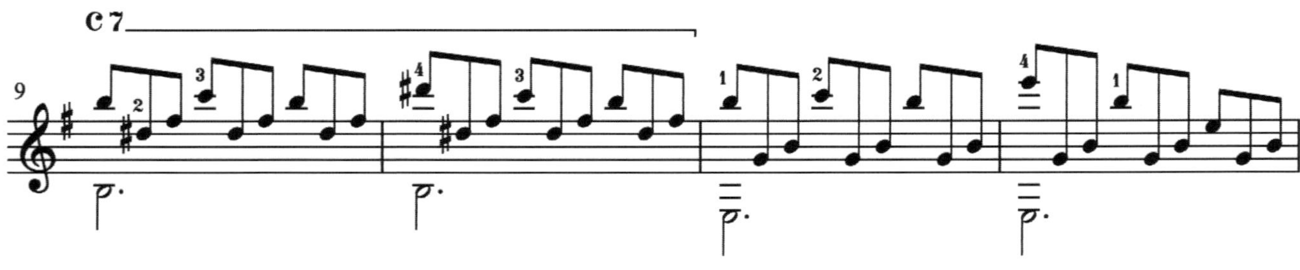

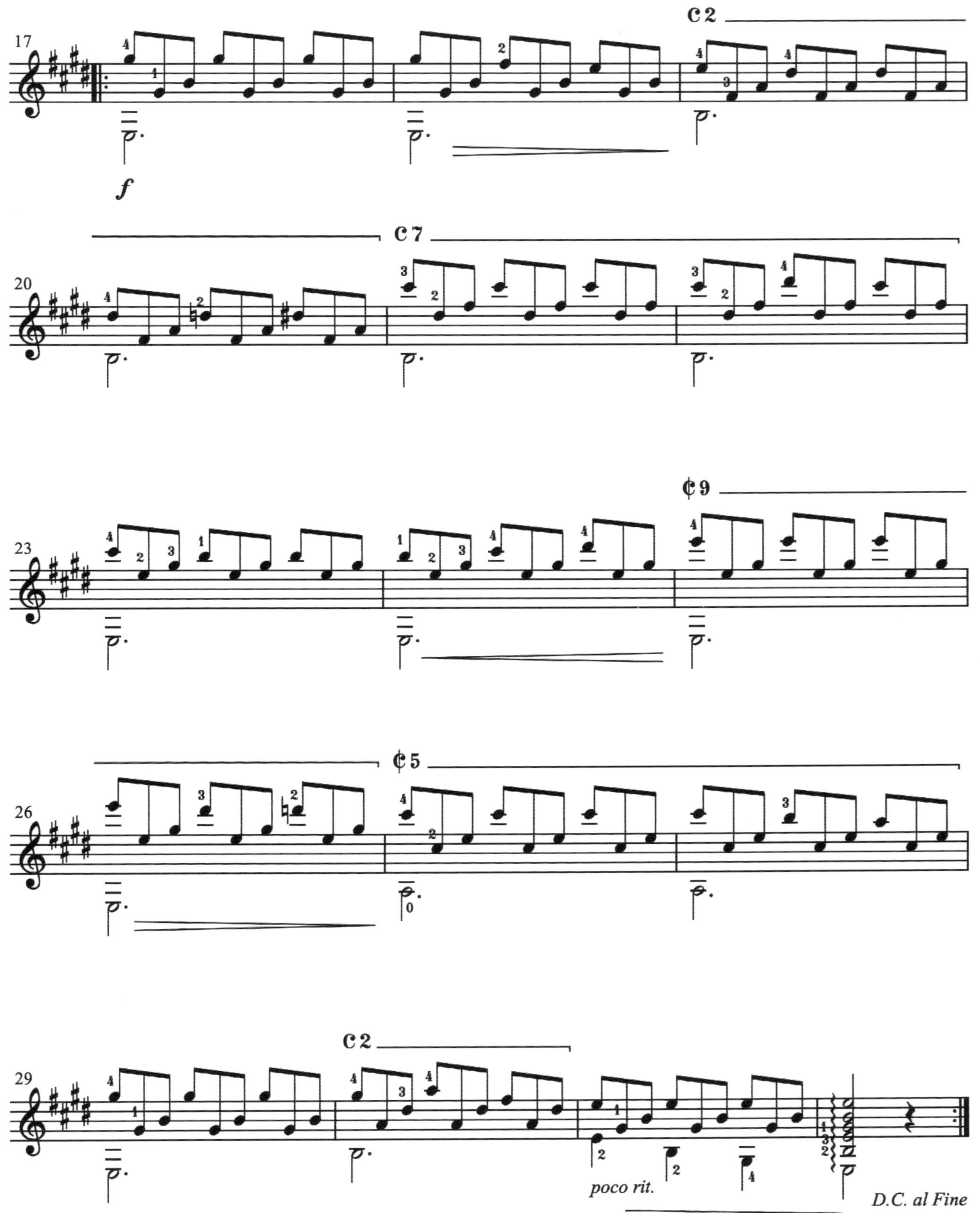
17
f
C2
20
C7
23
¢9
26
¢5
29
C2
poco rit.
D.C. al Fine

Two Guitars

Russian Folk Song

Anonymous

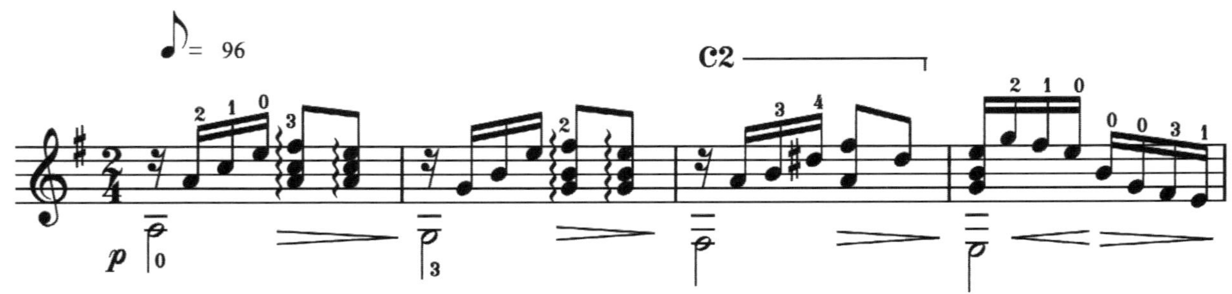

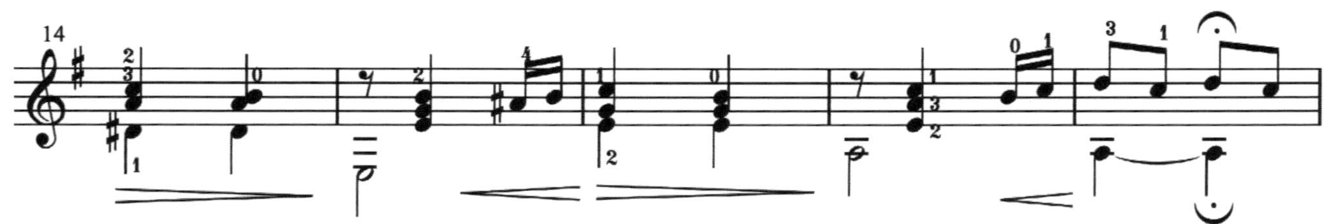

19
accell. poco a poco
23
♩ = 160
Fast and Animated
27
f
32
a
m
i
37
D.C. al Fine

Minuet

Excerpt from "Le Tombeau de Couperin"
Arr. by Paulo Oliveira

Maurice Ravel
(1875-1937)

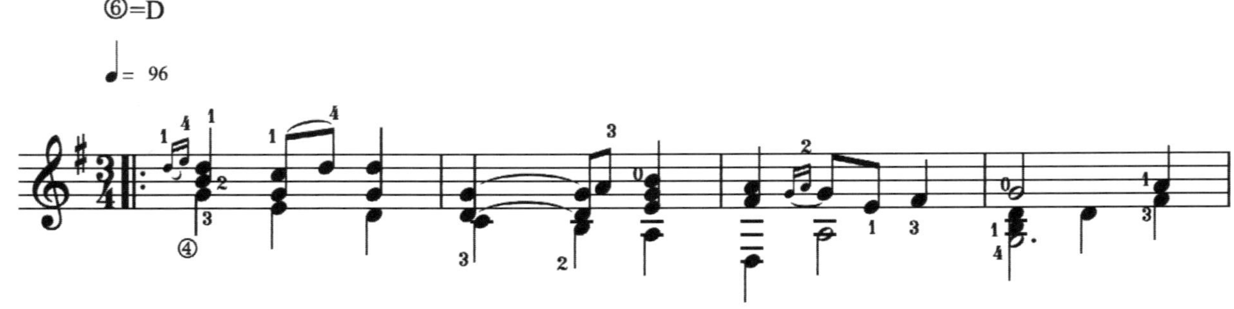

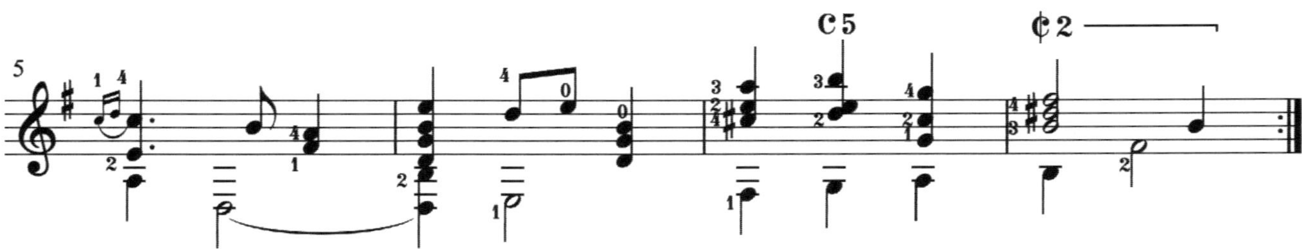

Juventude

Study no. 1

José Ricardo da Silva
(b. 1986)

11
m a m
i p i
i p
4 2
4
¢4
m a m
a m
13
i p i
¢2 ¢2 ¢2
3 3
4 3 0 1 4
3
15
3 3 3
2 3 4 4 4 2
0
3 1 1
2/4 C
Lento
Harm. 8va
17
i a m i a
4 0 4
C 8 3
p p p
1 2 3
D.C. al Fine
4
19
¢2 3 2
4 Harm. 8va
2/4 4 1
3 C 4
6 5
Fine

The First Flight of Asa Branca

Celso Delneri
(b. 1951)

Part V: Scales and Technical Exercises

"If you want to be the best you have to do the things
that others aren't prepared to do."
Michael Phelps

Open String Scales - First Position

These scales are meant to be played in first position: finger 1 for fret one, finger 2 for fret 2, finger 3 for fret 3, and finger 4 for fret 4.

For the right hand you should alternate i m or m i. You can also practice repeating each note twice to improve i m/m i alternation.

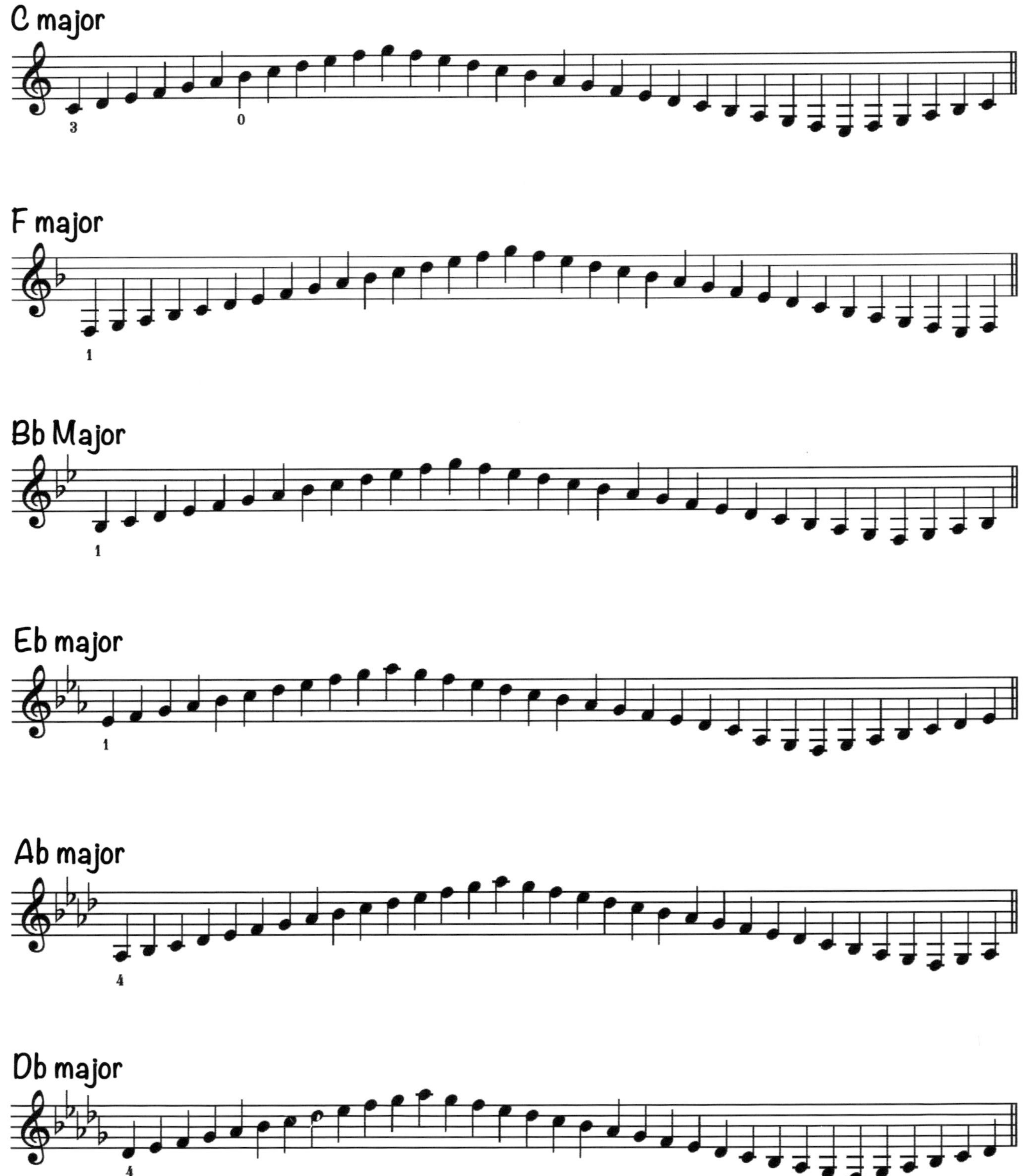

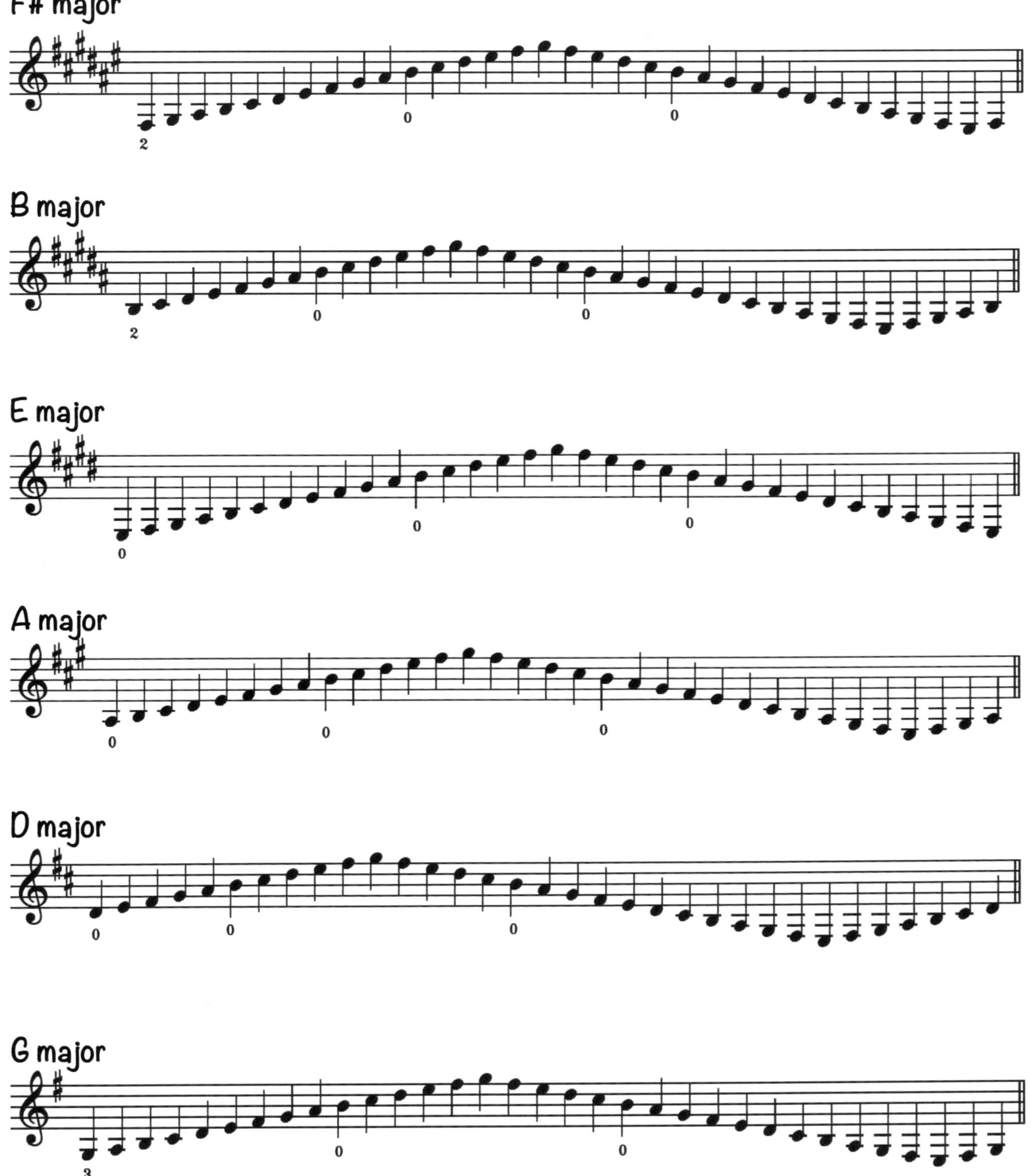

F# major
2
B major
2
E major
0
A major
0
D major
0
G major
3

3rds, 6ths, and 10ths

These exercises should be played in both descending and ascending forms.

D major

3rds

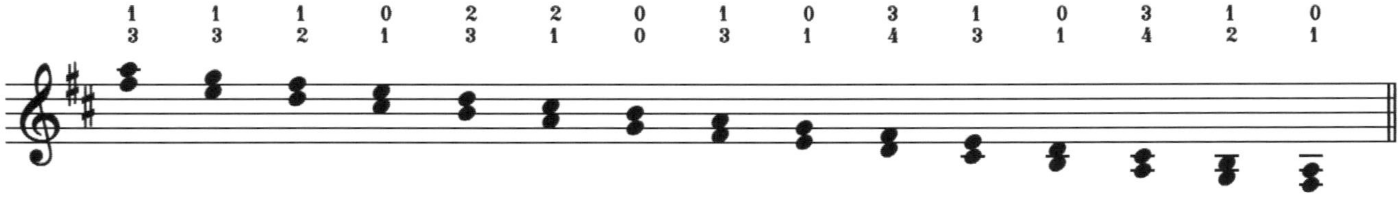

6ths

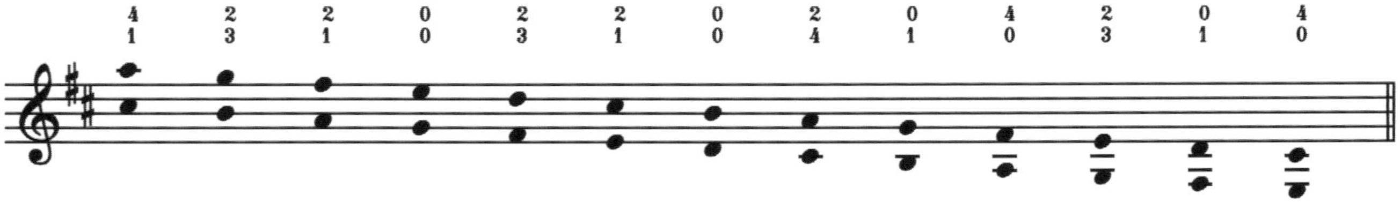

10ths

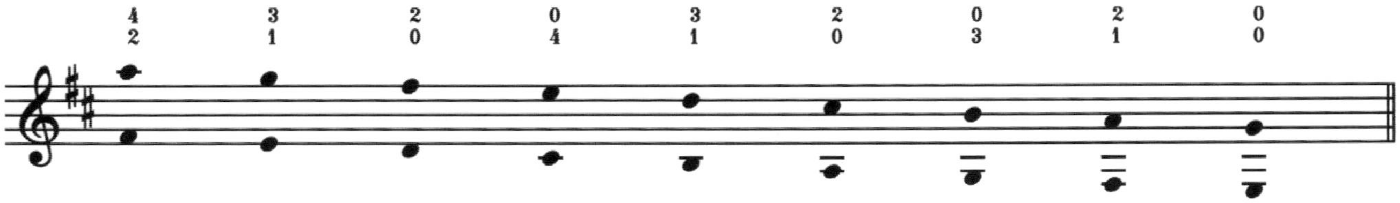

A major

3rds

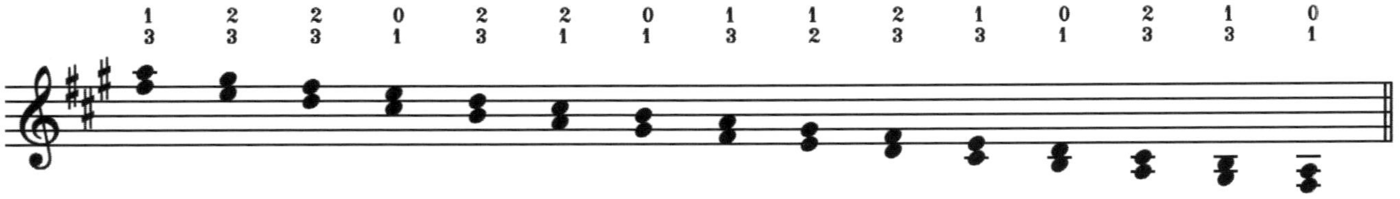

6ths

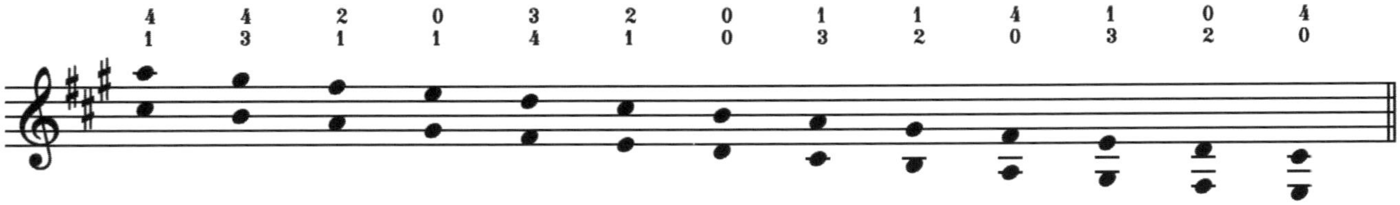

10ths

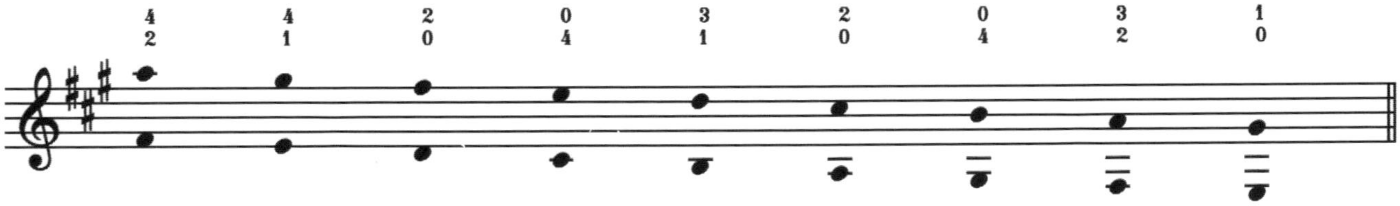

E major

3rds

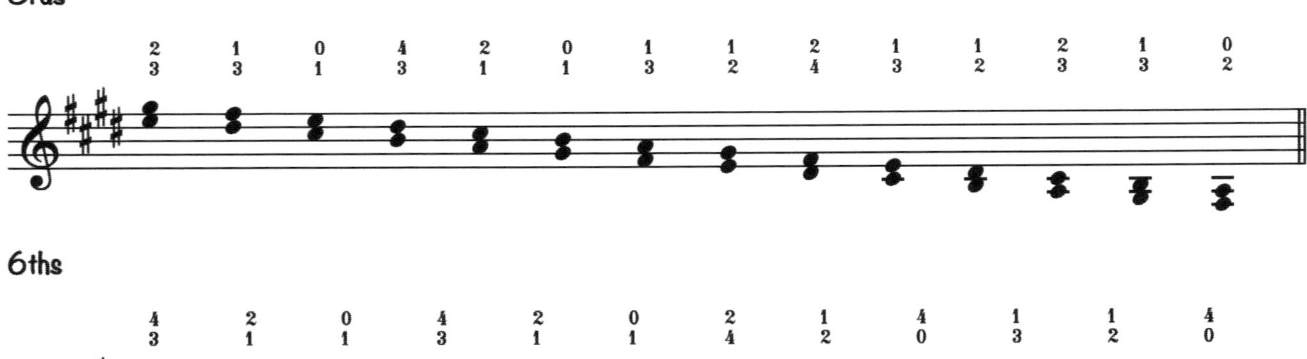

6ths

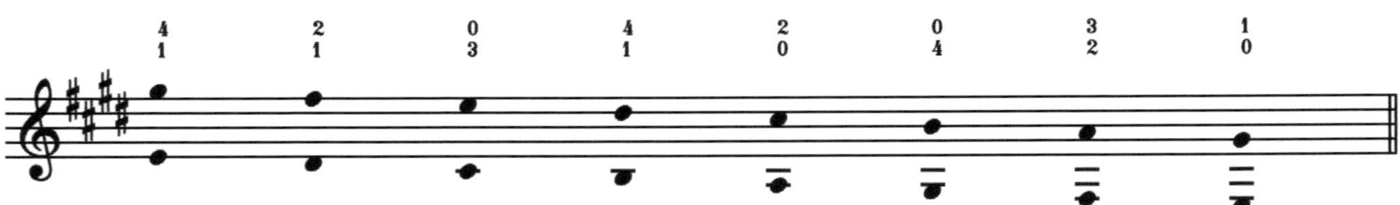

10ths

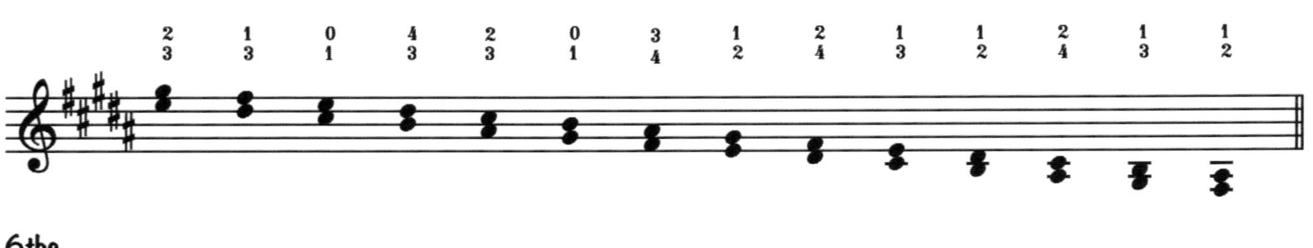

B major

3rds

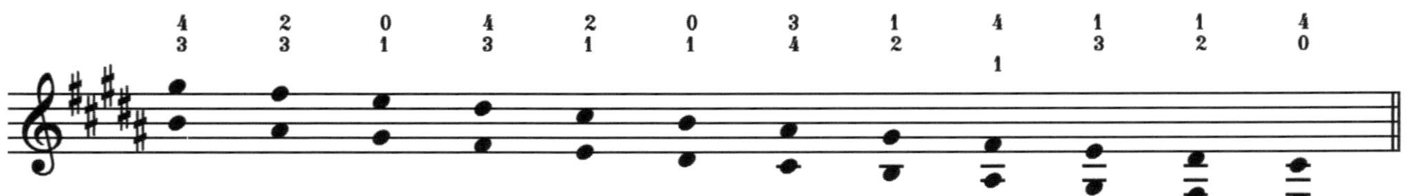

6ths

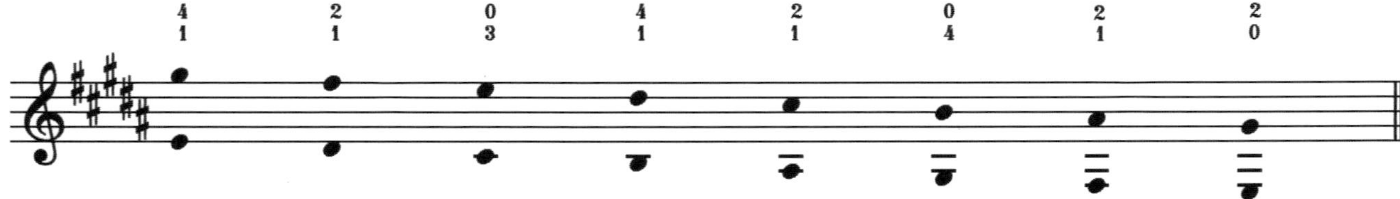

10ths

Chromatic Octaves

These exercises can be practiced with m i right hand fingering instead of i m.

Slur Exercises
Diatonic and Pentatonic Scales

Fifth Position

Fifth Position

Seventh Position

Seventh Position

Part VI: Comping Patterns and Three-Note Voicings

"Excellence is the gradual result of always
striving to do better."
Pat Riley

Major ii-V-I Comping Patterns

4/4 Swing
Bass notes should not overlap
Fingerings with no open strings

3/4 Swing

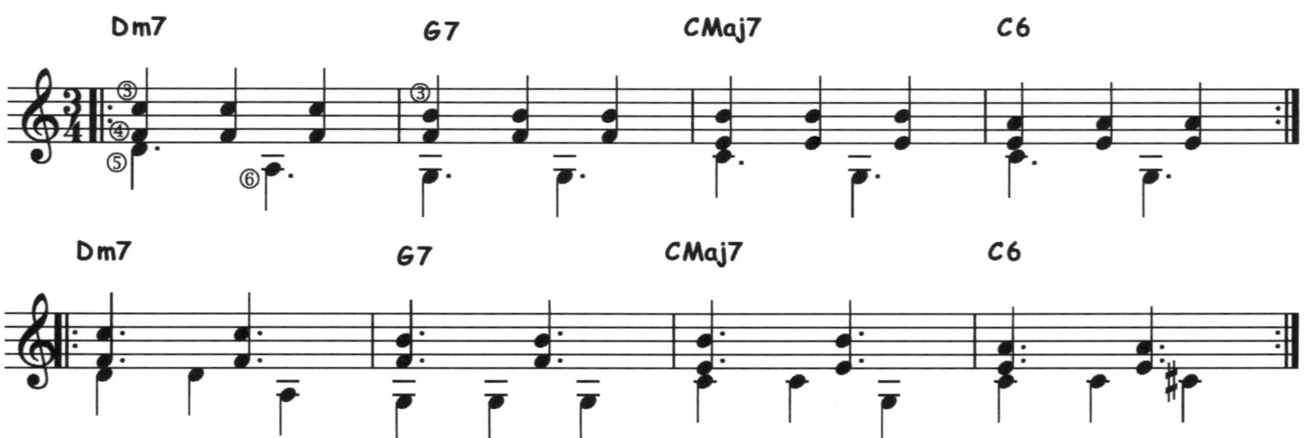

Bossa Nova (even 8th notes)

*The upper voices can also be played with a short duration.

*The last bossa example works well as a samba when played at a fast tempo

Minor ii-V-i Comping Patterns

4/4 Swing

3/4 Swing

Bossa Nova (even 8th notes)

Walking Blues

I have limited the rhythmic patterns to three styles: 4/4 swing, 3/4 swing, and bossa nova. These written patterns are just a point of departure. Once the student learns a few different patterns of each style he/she should work on creating rhythmic variations. I also limited the chords to three-note voicings (1, 3, 7, also known as shell voicings) in a few different keys. These examples provide two different shapes that can easily be transposed to all twelve keys. As soon as the student becomes comfortable with these exercises, I would urge him/her to apply these chord voicings and rhythmic patterns to jazz and bossa nova standards. The earlier the student is able to apply these concepts to real music the better.

A few examples of standards for practice would be: "All The Things You Are," "Beautiful Love," "There Will Never Be Another You," "Fly Me to the Moon," "Autumn Leaves," "My Favorite Things," "Stella by Starlight," "Invitation," "Have You Met Ms. Jones," "Misty," "Blue in Green," "Blue Monk," "Someday My Prince Will Come," "Bluesette," "Girl From Ipanema," "Summer Samba," "Blue Bossa," among others.

Major ii – V – I Progressions in all Keys

In order to become fluent with these three-note voicings and rhythmic patterns, it is important to practice them in all keys. A great benefit of practicing this progression in the cycle of fourths, is the fact that one must use both ii-V-I shapes: the one with the root on the fifth string and the one with the root on the sixth string. That way, the voicings will be close to each other during the key change.

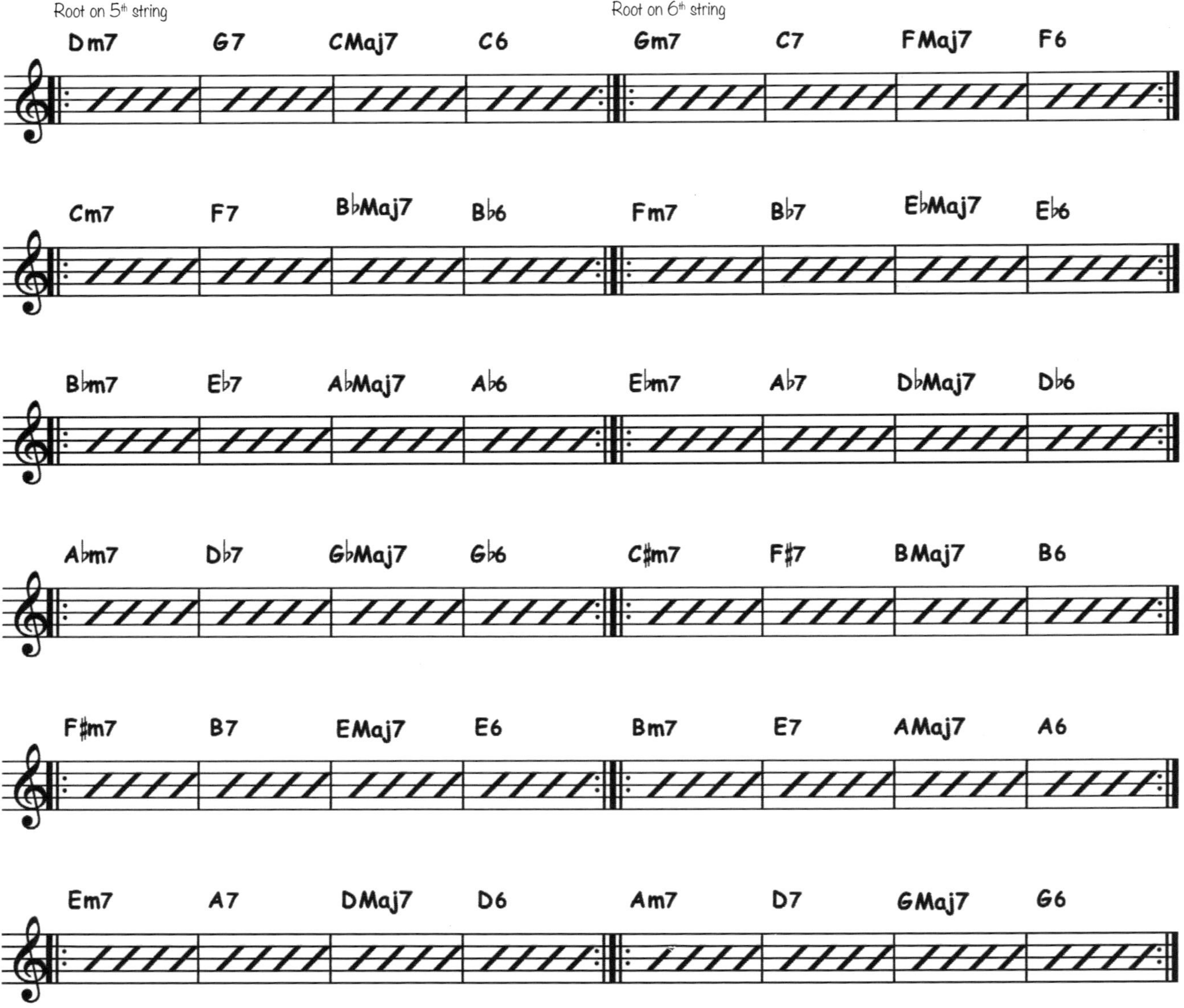